Alphabet Soup

**A Recipe for Understanding and Treating
Attention Deficit (Hyperactivity) Disorder**

ADD/ADHD

A Handbook for Parents and Teachers

James Javorsky, M.ED.

Minerva Press, Inc.
Clarkston, MI

Published by:
Minerva Press, Inc.
6653 Andersonville Road
Clarkston, MI 48346
1-(800)-423-3764

Forward

It is not often that a book is written by a professional from the view point of both patient and clinician. I found this handbook to be very informative. This manual provides practical information to concerned individuals who are addressing the special problems and needs of children, adolescent, and adults with ADD/ADHD. This handbook is written in a manner which parents, educators, and clinical professionals can all follow in an organized and concise form.

James Javorsky, M.Ed., has given us all a look inside the mind of a person with this disorder as well as a road map to follow in treating persons that are affected by ADD/ADHD. The author is explicit, practical, and sensitive to the needs of the parent, educator, and affected person as well as the clinical professional.

Alphabet Soup is a wonderful contribution to the field of ADD/ADHD and I highly recommend it to all concerned individuals.

Debora Ferguson, M.D.
Child and Adult Psychiatrist
Bloomfield Hills, Michigan

Introduction

Personally and professionally, I have experienced and witnessed the challenges of attention deficit hyperactivity disorder (ADHD). As an elementary special education teacher, university counselor, and school director at a psychiatric hospital, I have seen the damaging effects of ADD on families, adults, adolescents, and children. Most importantly, I am diagnosed with both attention deficit hyperactivity disorder and dyslexia - specific language learning disability. During my childhood, I spent summers fighting my peers or playing alone. In elementary and middle school, I daydreamed my way through classes and manipulated my teachers. Due to my social difficulties, I "missed" all the dating and extracurricular events, such as proms and homecomings.

In order to compensate for my learning difficulties, I cheated my way through high school (microfilm cheat sheets) and college (skipping exams). As an adult, I excessively used caffeine during the day and alcohol during the evening/night in order to fulfill my responsibilities at home and work.

I hardly considered that my disabilities or differences were considered barriers or obstacles to my future successes. I have always been ADHD and dyslexic and I will always be ADHD and dyslexic. I do not know the difference. Given medication, remediation, support, and therapy, I have found my recipe for success. I have published over twelve articles in educational and research journals on learning disabilities. I have made numerous presentations on learning disabilities and attention deficit hyperactivity disorders at local, regional, national, and international conferences and organizations. I have held local and national leadership positions in the Orton Dyslexia Society, Learning Disabilities Association, and Children with Attention Deficit Disorder Association. I have been an elementary special education teacher, university counselor, director of a tutorial and peer counseling program at a major psychiatric hospital. I wish to thank my wife, Teresa, parents, and professionals for believing in me and showing me how to unlock my potential.

Drawing upon my personal insight, professional training and research in the field of ADD, this introductory handbook was written primarily for parents and teachers and should not be used as a substitute for assessment and treatment by trained professionals. This handbook is one of the first steps in becoming a wise consumer in this field. Parents are encouraged to learn as much on ADD as possible and to ask questions of professionals in order to become knowledgeable and cautious consumers.

This handbook is dedicated to the parents of children and adolescents with ADD. Sharing their children's frustration, confusion, and successes, parents are challenged to find the secrets of "making alphabet soup". Through mixing love, respect, teaching, understanding, and discipline, children with ADD learn their own recipe for success.

Table of Contents

Another school day begins for Jimmy, a twelve year old child who has ADD/ADHD* (Attention Deficit Disorder or Attention Deficit Hyperactivity Disorder). He was diagnosed in the fourth grade and has received the best the school has to offer to teach him how to behave at home and in school. Every day Jimmy struggles to maintain his self esteem; however, school and home pose many personal challenges. Each morning he boards the school bus and sits alone because the other children think he is strange. Being easily distracted and confused, Jimmy feels like he is in a never ending maze when he leaves his bus, goes to his locker and enters his classroom. Every day he manages to walk into class late and disorganized. The teacher asks the class to turn in the homework which Jimmy forgot at home or in his locker. Without his homework, Jimmy is scolded by the teacher for being "lazy and insubordinate." He thinks that if he only knew what insubordinate means he would be able to find a way to please his teacher and do his homework.

The teacher begins her lesson by talking non-stop for thirty minutes. Jimmy feels confused and lost throughout the lesson. Not only does he wish for the teacher to use smaller words and shorter sentences, but he longs for the teacher to answer his questions.

After thirty minutes of being confused, Jimmy finds sitting still very difficult. He moves and fidgets around in his chair. He looks for distractions, something to occupy his bored mind. No longer able to control himself, Jimmy talks out and wanders about the classroom. After the teacher's redirection, Jimmy's name goes on the board just like every other day. The children giggle and laugh as the teacher reminds Jimmy to remain quiet and stay in his seat. The teacher finishes her lesson and hands out work to the children. While each of the children complete the work in ten minutes, Jimmy stares out the window, because he did not hear the directions or the assignment.

After several classes, Jimmy goes to lunch. He is told by the other children what to buy with his lunch money. The children giggle and laugh as Jimmy purchases five Twinkees. Because he has

---

*The terms ADD and ADHD are used interchangeably in this article.

not completely mastered table manners, Jimmy ends up wearing most of his lunch in his lap and on his face. While the children laugh at him, Jimmy thinks he is winning their friendship. The teacher sees his mess and asks him to clean the cafeteria while the other children are on the playground. As he wipes the tables, he thinks that cleaning is better than playing since no one wants to play with him.

Finally, Jimmy boards the school bus to return home with a letter to his parents concerning his next after-school detention.

His whole learning for the school day amounted to one hour with his tutor who helped him understand the math lesson. For the remainder of the day, Jimmy was teased, ignored, isolated, scolded, and hurt by his peers and teachers. Jimmy tries to remember the positive comments of his tutor and parents, but he only remembers the confusion, frustration, and anger that he has about his differences. Filled with energy and anger, Jimmy leaves the school bus and finds one of the children who was teasing him earlier in the day. After a few minutes of name calling, Jimmy and the other child exchange punches and kicks, and then Jimmy limps home with torn pants, a bloody nose, and hurt feelings.

When he gets home, bruised and dirty, Jimmy turns on his Nintendo and plays alone for hours. His parents scold him for the mess he left in his room that morning and Jimmy tells his parents, "You never told me to clean it." These words fall upon the floor as his parents send him to bed early. As he falls asleep, he dreams of what life would be like if he was "normal and whole" like the rest of the children.

Jimmy is not real, yet he could be any number of children with ADD. His learning differences are at constant war with his emotions, behaviors, and school performance. Children like Jimmy are at risk for the development of significant emotional and behavioral disorders.

As a psychiatric hospital school director and ADD specialist, I see children whose worlds are torn apart emotionally and educationally because of their differences. Furthermore, I was diagnosed LD in the first grade and ADD as an adult, so Jimmy's life may be a reflection of my childhood. In this book, I will discuss symptoms, causes, diagnosis, and emotional, social, and behavioral difficulties of ADD and offer suggestions for appropriate interventions.

Characteristics of Attention Deficit Disorder

The three core symptoms or traits which most experts say characterize ADD are: 1) Difficulties with persistence of effort (sustained attention); 2) Impulsivity (behavioral disinhibition); and 3) Hyperactivity (behavioral regulation and control). Russell Barkley, one of the nation's leading researchers in the field of ADD, reports that children with ADD may "lag" 30% behind in comparison with their peers in these three areas. In addition, children with ADD may exhibit the following additional characteristics of ADD: Emotional over-arousal; difficulties in delaying gratification; and difficulties with rule-governed behavior.

Difficulties with Persistence of Effort (Sustained Attention)

Children with ADD have difficulties sustaining their attention on tasks which they perceive as routine, tedious, and repetitive. In order to sustain attention or persistence, the activity needs to be of high interest or have high severe negative consequences. The diagnosis of ADD does not suggest that the child has generalized attention disorder; however, the disorder may be situation specific in relation to the environment and to the task. Consequently, children with ADD may appear one day to be very attentive and persistent while the next day to be very distractible depending upon the environment and/or the task.

Impulsivity (Behavioral Disinhibition)

Children with ADD tend to act without considering the consequences of their actions. They seem to have difficulties with inhibiting their behavioral responses to stimuli. Children with ADD are likely to respond at the moment rather than delaying their responses in order to consider the consequences of their actions. Impulsivity or behavioral disinhibition, according to some researchers, is the most defining characteristic of this disorder. ADD is not a skills based deficit, but a performance deficit. In other words, children with ADD may understand how to plan and organize their time, but they may lack the behavioral control to use such a plan.

Hyperactivity (Behavioral Regulation/Control)

Due to their difficulties with behavioral inhibition and sustained attention (persistence of effort), children with ADD appear to be hyperverbal or hyperactive. This characteristic may appear given a certain context (environment or task) such as completing an essay or doing paperwork. Their work or academic performance will appear to have a significant amount of variability. Not only does hyperactivity relate to physical movement, it may also appear in their thoughts and conversations. In the classroom, living room, or school cafeteria, children with ADD may appear to be fidgety, squirmy, day dreamy, overly verbal and socially intrusive.

Emotional Over-arousal

Children with ADD tend to be overly "expressive" in sharing their feelings with parents, teachers, and friends. These children may be prone to acting out their emotions physically and/or verbally by fighting, swearing, arguing, and complaining. From anger to happiness, children with ADD may experience the peaks and valleys of these emotions. Riding on an emotional roller coaster, they tend to be unpredictable and inconsistent with their moods when interacting with other people. At times, they may show significant difficulties in separating feelings from content in conversations. Children with ADD are likely to interpret and generalize the statements of others as a personal affront and respond accordingly to such a statement. This characteristic will likely hurt their ability to make and maintain friendships.

Difficulty with Delaying Gratification

Children with ADD may appear to be impatient. They may become angry and/or frustrated when faced with situations in which they have to wait. This may lead to acting-out behavior, defiance toward authority, or stealing/cheating behaviors. Standing in lines at amusement parks, waiting for food at a restaurant, and playing team sports may be affected by this characteristic. Holidays and birthdays may pose problems for children with ADD because they have to wait for the "special" day in order to receive their gifts and presents.

Difficulties with Rule-Governed Behavior

Given the core symptoms of ADD, it is not surprising to find that these children have difficulties in complying with rules. They may have difficulty in following school, parent, and/or social rules. For example, these children may cheat on tests or homework, ignore curfews, break promises, fail to complete chores, and show poor sportsmanship. They may know the rules and consequences for their behavior; however, this disorder affects their ability to comply with the rules. Given these difficulties, these children may not fully develop an appropriate understanding of social interactions and skills. Being aggressive, impulsive, and uninhibited, they may encounter difficulties fitting in with peer groups and are often social outcasts who seek and desire social acceptance. The social skills which children with ADD develop may focus on ways to manipulate peers and adults in order to satisfy their own needs and wants.

Cause of Attention Deficit Disorder

Children with ADD live with an invisible disability, one that is real, however, sometimes hard to prove by medical, psychological, or educational testing. Misunderstood by teachers and parents, children with ADD may be criticized and scolded because they do not behave appropriately at home and at school. Unfortunately, some parents and teachers believe that children with ADD are making choices to misbehave and that "just good old fashioned discipline" is all that is needed to correct these behaviors. Reasoning such as this will only cause further emotional and behavioral difficulties for children with ADD. Several theories have developed concerning the causes of ADD. First, bad parenting does not cause ADD; yet appropriate parenting skills may lessen the difficulties of children with ADD. Second, foods (sugar) and allergies do not cause ADD; however, they may aggravate or exaggerate the characteristics of ADD. Finally, brain damage may explain only a small percentage of ADD cases. It is estimated that only 10% of children with ADD show hard evidence of brain damage. Children with emotional disorders, such as depression, do exhibit some qualities of inattention and distractibility, however, these children are not considered ADD because their inattentiveness is caused by an emotional disorder.

According to research, current thinking favors the theory that ADD is a biochemical imbalance within the brain. There appears to be a deficiency in the brain's ability to produce chemicals which are called "transmitter substances" or neurotransmitters. These chemicals form a communication system for the regulation of behavior. The current theory is that there is a shortage of these chemicals (neurotransmitters) within the brain. This results in the brain being under-stimulated and weak in managing its own activities such as attention, concentration, and impulsivity. Research has suggested that ADD is hereditary. It has been estimated that 50% of fathers of children with ADD and 25-30% of the siblings of children with ADD be ADD themselves. Parents of children with ADD tend to show higher incidence than the population of several other problems, such as alcoholism, depression, hysteria, psychosis, and sociopathology. In turn, these children and families seem to be prone to emotional and behavior problems than the rest of the population.

Emotional and Social Aspects of Attention Deficit Disorder

Due to their differences in learning and/or behavior, children with ADD may develop negative feelings about themselves and their abilities. Typically, these children may have difficulty with the following:

1. Developing a positive self concept and a sense of security and competence
2. Being over dependent upon teachers and parents
3. Establishing self-confidence
4. Accepting criticism
5. Tolerating frustration
6. Trusting others
7. Acting maturely

8. Developing appropriate morals and values
9. Maintaining motivation
10. Controlling anxiety

In addition, children with ADD may have difficulty appropriately interacting with peers and adults. These difficulties may hinder the development of appropriate social skills, such as the following:

1. Establishing good relationships and working appropriately with others
2. Developing appropriate family relationships
3. Understanding body language and facial expressions
4. Controlling impulsive comments during conversations
5. Stating their feelings and thoughts
6. Knowing what to say in a situation
7. Understanding humor and sarcasm
8. Using appropriate personal hygiene and table manners
9. Relating to authority figures and adults
10. Understanding and building relationships with peers.

Consequently, children with ADD without appropriate interventions may be prone to developing characteristics of severe psychiatric disorders, such as oppositional-defiant disorder or depression. These feelings may deepen, leading to possible substance abuse, self harm, or verbal and physical conflicts with parents and peers.

Diagnosis of Attention Deficit Disorder

According to researchers and professionals in the field, there is no one test that can be used to determine whether a child is or is not definitely ADD. The diagnostic process is usually based on a multidisciplinary or diagnostic team approach. Members of the team may include parents, teacher, educational psychologist, clinical psychologist, social worker, psychiatrist, nurse, and pediatrician. The diagnosis of ADD is like detective work. A diagnostic team gathers the clues which may be based upon test data, interviews, observation, and rating scales. Based upon these clues, the diagnostic team decides on the appropriate diagnosis and designs a treatment program for the child.

The assessment, which is usually based on the following components, is summarized in the following list:

Parent Interview
- Child's characteristics, traits, and symptoms
- Developmental history
- Medical history
- School history
- Family development, social, medical, and mental health history

Child Interview
- Child's behavior and symptoms
- Child's awareness and explanation of difficulties
- Screening for other disorders, such as depression or anxiety

Psychological Assessment
- Measures of general intelligence and cognition
- Personality and emotional testing

Psychoeducational and Language Assessment
- Measures of educational and language skills, reading, mathematics, written and oral language, and thinking and reasoning
- Observation of social and pragmatic skills

Medical Evaluation
- Determination of general health status
- Screening for sensory deficits, neurological deficits, or other physical explanations of difficulties

Teacher and Parent Rating Scales
- Broad measures to screen for social, behavioral and emotional difficulties

Parent Interview

The parent interview provides important information concerning the child's emotional, social, and behavioral problems. Generally, parents are asked to describe their concerns about the child and when, where, how often, and with whom these behaviors are observed. Detailed information about the child's developmental, medical, and school history are gathered. In addition, background information is obtained concerning the family's social, medical, and mental health history - not just for determining the presence of ADD but for revealing any other possible causes for the observed behaviors. Finally, the parents may be asked to give permission to the interviewer in order to obtain school and health records. These records may assist the interviewer in evaluating the child's developmental and educational history.

Child Interview

The child interview reveals information concerning the child's understanding of their difficulties. When placed in a new setting or environment, a child, whether ADD or not, is more subdued in their behavior and emotion and behaves more appropriately in one-to-one situations. Consequently, an interview may provide an inaccurate or incomplete profile of the child's attention deficits. Usually, the interviewer assesses the child's perceptions of their academic, social, emotional and/or behavioral difficulties at home and/or in school. It is also important to ask the child whether he/she has experienced symptoms of depression, anxiety, or distorted thinking. The interviewer may engage the child in a play or game activity in order to determine the child's level of attention, distractibility, and impulsivity in an activity of high interest. Finally, the interviewer may ask the child to read a passage or write a story in order to evaluate the child's focus for educational tasks.

Psychological Testing

Psychological testing reveals the child's intellectual or cognitive functioning. This provides information about whether the child has the aptitude to complete the tasks which are being asked of him/her. One of the most commonly used, individually administered tests, is the Wechsler Intelligence Scales for Children-III. This test is designed to measure the child's intelligence or aptitude, but it can not diagnose ADD. Sometimes the Freedom from Distractibility Scale, which is derived from the test results, has been used to screen for ADD. Research suggests that the low scores of this scale do not indicate whether or not the child has ADD.

A projective or personality assessment may be administered to evaluate the emotional and behavioral status of the child. This information may assist the team in determining the origin and severity of the child's emotional difficulties. Also, psychological testing may reveal that the child has a co- occurring or separate emotional disorder which may require specific therapy or medication other than the options used for ADD.

Educational and Language Testing

Since approximately 15-20% of children with learning language disabilities (LDD) have ADD, an assessment of the child's educational and language abilities provides information concerning cognitive and educational abilities. Researchers have determined that a learning/language disability may be the result of genetic or inborn difference in the cell organization of the language section of the brain. Consequently, this difference affects the child's abilities in the areas of reading, mathematics, written language, speaking, and/or listening skills. An educational assessment may determine whether the child's school difficulties are caused by a learning disability, attention deficit disorder, or a combination of both disorders. The most widely used educational assessment is the Woodcock Johnson Revised Tests of Achievement. This test measures children's reading, mathematics, written language, and knowledge, however, it does not diagnose ADD. In the areas of written language, additional testing may be required to determine the child's strengths and weaknesses. The Test of Written Language - 2, which is a measure of a child's writing skills in both structured and unstructured situations, may be a useful test for a child with ADD. Because he/she has difficulties with organization and planning, the child with ADD may have difficulty performing on written language tests which require the child to develop their own structure. A language assessment provides information concerning the child's receptive and expressive language skills and social skills. If the child has difficulty in learning or language, the child may appear inattentive or distractible, because he/she does not understand the task.

Since children with ADD tend to have significant difficulties with social skills, the Test of Language Competence - Expanded Edition, which measures the child's oral language and pragmatic (social) skills, may provide useful information which may assist parents and teachers in understanding and addressing the child's social skills weaknesses. A Parent's Guide to Educational and Intelligence Tests (Appendix A) and A Parent's Guide to Test Results (Appendix B) are included in this book.

Medical Evaluation

A child who is presenting symptoms of ADD should have an appropriate medical evaluation. Medical problems, such as vision or hearing deficits, tic disorders, or other neurological conditions may be causing the observed behavioral difficulties. Children with ADD undergoing medication treatment will continue to need careful medical observation. This information may be shared with the school nurse in order to assist in the monitoring of medication and behavior.

Parent and Teacher Rating Scales

Rating scales which may be administered by pediatricians, social workers, teachers, or psychologist, are usually used to screen children who are suspected of having ADD. The following are some of the most commonly used rating scales:

Conners Parent and Teacher Rating Scales
Attention Deficit Disorders Evaluation Scales (School and Home)
ADD-H Comprehensive Teacher's Rating Scale (ACTeRS)

Significant adults in the child's life, parents and/or teachers, are asked to complete a form which assesses the presence and absence of specific behaviors. These scales, which are easy to administer and grade, provide information concerning the child's behaviors. On the other hand, rating scales are vulnerable to influence by positive or negative "halo effects." Halo effects are the natural tendency for human beings to be influenced by outside factors, such as one's feelings and temperament that day or one's long standing perceptions and beliefs about the child. If the child is social and warm, the halo effect may be positive. If the child is aggressive and impulsive, the halo effect may be negative. Furthermore, rating scales assume that the rater has adequate experience with the child. If a parent or teacher seldom interacts with the child, the results may be an incomplete view of the child's behaviors. Consequently, rating scales are an appropriate screening test for ADD but ought not be relied upon for diagnosis.

Home Interventions for Attention Deficit Disorder

Parenting a child with ADD might be compared to taming and managing a tornado. Always on the go and acting on impulse, the child with ADD may cause turmoil and chaos within even the most stable home. At times the parents may be in conflict over discipline and management of the child. Attempting to correct the child's behavior, parents may enter an ineffective cycle of feedback, such as the following: l) reasoning with the child, 2) persuading the child, 3) yelling at the child, and 4) hitting the child. This cycle often leads to breakdowns in communication between child and parent. The child and parent develop a negative relationship which is grounded in anger and punishment. The child may become oppositional and defiant against the parent and, in turn, the parent may become harsh and hateful with the child. The following recommendations are suggestions to help manage a child with ADD at home:

1. The 1-2-3 behavior management system (Phelan, 1992, see references) has been found effective for children with ADD. The purpose of the 1-2-3 behavior management system is to avoid arguing about the child's behavior and debating the punishment. It is designed to provide immediate behavioral consequences that have proven to be effective in child management. If the behavior is inappropriate, state the behavior and why it is inappropriate. If behavior continues, say to the child "That's 1;" if the behavior continues, "That's 2;" if the behavior continues, "That's 3 and

take a five minute time-out." If the initial inappropriate behavior is serious (fighting), state, "That's 3 and take a five (or possibly ten) minute time-out". The time out center should be a place in the home which is removed from the traffic pattern free of distractions, such as the laundry room or bathroom (assuring that both of these rooms are child proof). A timer is set for the time-out period once the inappropriate behavior has ceased and the child is quiet and calm. After time-out is served, avoid talking about the incident.

2. Design, with the child, the rules, expectations, and consequences of behavior at home. This list should be posted in a visible place. A contract system with reward menus may assist the parents and child in defining appropriate expectations. Rewards may need to be real, substantial, and frequent in order to insure the child's compliance.

3. Provide an appropriate and consistent study area. This space should be designed to allow the child to study in an area of the house which is away from distractions, such as TV or family members.

4. Implement a daily homework time. With the child's input, parents set a homework time (for example, 4:00 p.m. - 5:00 p.m.) each day for the child. During this time, a timer should be set for fifteen to thirty minutes of study, then a five minute break. This will help the child pace his study efforts.

5. Provide assistance, when necessary, with class assignments.

6. Assist the child in the organization of the child's materials prior to school and after school, such as helping with book bags or back packs.

7. Support the teacher's rules and consequences for the child.

8. Work cooperatively and positively with the school, teachers and administrators, in designing and implementing an educational and behavioral program which provides appropriate and reasonable accommodations (listed in the following School Interventions section).

9. Reinforce the usage of age-appropriate social skills at home, such as no swearing or fighting.

10. Provide the school, teachers and administrators, with testing or documentation concerning the child's diagnosis and treatment recommendations.

11. Provide the school personnel with information from the child's physician concerning medication: usage, dosage, and side effects. Assure that the school has an ample amount of medication for the child.

Working with their child, the parents may foster the foundation of respect and discipline which may improve the communication and reinforce appropriate behavior with the child. Consequently, the parents and the child develop a supportive relationship which will provide the basis for school success.

School Interventions for Attention Deficit Disorder

Children with ADD face many challenges within the school environment. Constant changes, time-based homework, tests, lectures and note-taking, sitting for hours, teasing and ridicule from peers and teachers, and low grades are sources of frustration, anger, and confusion for children with ADD. Some children with ADD and significant learning or emotional difficulties receive special education services. Individual's with Disabilities Education's Act (IDEA) is the law which defines guidelines and services for children who require special education. Children with ADD may be identified and serviced under one of several categories of special education, including (I) emotionally impaired/severe behavioral handicapped, (2) specific learning disabilities, or (3) otherwise health impaired. Under special education law, the school is obliged to evaluate, design, and implement an individual education plan (IEP) for each child with a certified disability. The IEP functions as a contract between the school and the parents concerning the education of the child.

ADD is a handicap/disability as defined by Section 504 of the Civil Rights Act of 1973. This legislation states that "no institution receiving federal money can discriminate on the basis of a handicap". Consequently, schools are obliged to provide "reasonable" accommodations and support for a child with ADD. These accommodations are typically changes or modifications in instruction and/or testing. Section 504 does not mandate "special programs or services" for children with ADD and assumes that the child should receive accommodations in a "regular" or normal learning environment.

Not all children with ADD require special education services. It has been estimated that 75% of children with ADD will remain in regular education and succeed with assistance and accommodations. These accommodations are based upon Section 504 of the Civil Rights Act of 1973. These accommodations should benefit the child with ADD and assist the teacher in meeting the educational and behavioral needs of all their students.

The following are accommodations which may be implemented in regular or special classroom settings:

Classroom Accommodations

1. Design a seating arrangement which allows for teacher movement and minimal distractions from classmates.
2. Place the child near the teacher's desk.
3. Locate the child's desk away from both hallways and windows in order to minimize distractions.
4. Stand near the child when giving directions or presenting a lesson. Use the child's work sheet as an example.
5. Place the classroom rules in a visible and accessible area.
6. Minimize room distractions such as air conditioners, fans, radios, and heaters.
7. Establish a daily classroom routine and schedule which is posted and follow the routine.

Instructional Accommodations:

1. Provide an outline or overview of lesson.
2. Vary the speed of the lesson.
3. Design brief lessons and divide longer lessons in smaller parts.
4. Employ a multisensory instructional method with various types of activity during each lesson.

    a. At times, have the child be an instructional aide during lessons and repeat/re-explain directions to class.

    b. Instruct the child to develop mental images of information being presented.

    c. Use role playing activities to act out key concepts.

    d. Use cooperative learning activities with preassigned roles and responsibilities.

5. Pair the child to work with a role model child in the class.

6. Provide peer tutoring to review lesson.

7. Use colors, materials, pictures, words, and objects when presenting new information.

8. Maintain eye contact with child during verbal instructions.

9. Make directions clear and concise. Be consistent with directions. Avoid directions with several steps.

10. Assess the child's comprehension of directions before beginning the task.

11. Repeat directions in a calm, positive manner, when necessary.

12. Allow the child access to teacher's lecture notes or note taking assistance.

Testing and Home/School Work Accommodations

1. Use large type. Papers which are difficult to read, such as blue ink dittos, may be troublesome for the child to complete.

2. Keep page format simple.

    a. Minimize visual distractions such as pictures that are unrelated to assignment.

    b. Have white space on each page.

3. Underline key directions or vocabulary words.

4. Divide work sheets into sections and assign only small sections.

5. Shorten assignments. If the child can demonstrate mastery in twenty questions, thirty to forty items may be inappropriate.

6. Use a tape recorder to record lessons and tests when necessary.

7. Provide an environment which is distraction free when the

child is completing a test.
8. Provide extended time for the child to complete a test.
9. Allow the child the opportunity, when necessary, to take tests orally or in an alternative method - papers and projects.
10. Insure that the child's knowledge of the subject is being tested and not the effects of attention deficit disorder.

Organizational Accommodations

1. Instruct the child on how to organize a desk and locker.
2. Allow the child five minutes daily to organize desk.
3. Use individual assignment charts or homework sheets which are sent home to the parent.
4. Develop a clear system for tracking homework - completed, incomplete, and missing assignments. These sheets may be sent home to parent.
5. Develop a reward system for in-school work and homework completion: Child receives token (raffle ticket, star) for an appropriate completion of homework. Start with rewarding completion and minimize accuracy. After child completes the work assigned, then reward quality and completion. Each token is saved for privileges or prizes.
6. Write schedule and time lines for assignments and projects on board.
7. Prepare the child for changes in activity by announcing to class when current activity is ending - "Five minutes to go."
8. Instruct the child on how to use a checklist which is taped on the child's desk or place in a folder. This checklist outlines the steps in following directions or completing assignment.
9. Provide study guides or outlines for the content that the child is expected to master.

Study/Home Accommodations

1. Support the parent's efforts in designing an appropriate learning setting at home. The child may benefit from an appropriate study space at home with routines established as far as set times for study, parental review of completed

homework, and periodic notebook and/or book bag organizer.

2. Instruct the child on how to use a calendar system so child will remember assignments and tests. This calendar may also include social and extracurricular activities.

Behavioral Accommodations

1. Design class rules to be clear and simple.
2. Define and review classroom rules each day at the start of the school year.
3. Allow the class to meet to discuss rules, privileges, rewards, and consequences for behavior - class meetings.
4. Reinforce appropriate behavior through classroom management and reward systems.
   a. Instruct the child how to self-monitor and self-reinforce.
   b. Use timer to indicate lengths of lesson and independent work times.
5. Set hourly, daily, weekly, and monthly goals with the child through a behavioral contract with child, parent, and teacher. Contract to specify the terms of behavior and subsequent consequences or rewards for changing behavior.
6. Provide a variety of rewards and privileges so that the child does not "burn out" on a particular reward. Adding an element of chance within the reward system provides variety.
7. Instruct other significant adults in the child's life on behavioral management system so that the adults are consistent with the terms, rewards, and consequences.
8. Allow the child to participate in deciding the consequences for their negative behaviors.
9. Implement the 1-2-3 behavior management system (Phelan, 1992; in reference section) at school (See Home Intervention section for complete description). If the initial inappropriate behavior is a serious infraction of school rules (fighting), state, "That's 3 and take a five (or possibly more, depending upon the severity of the incident) minute time-out." The time out center should be a seat in the classroom which is removed from the common traffic pattern of the class. A timer is set for the child when the child

is under control, quiet and calm. After time out is served, avoid talking about the incident.

Each child with ADD presents a different and unique profile of behaviors, emotions and educational skills. Some of these suggestions for school accommodations may assist the child in reaching their potential. However, the accommodations listed above may not be appropriate for every child with ADD. Working with school personnel, teachers and administrators, the parent may be able to facilitate the development an individual educational and behavioral plan which would be tailored for the child's abilities and differences.

Collaborative Interventions for Attention Deficit Disorder

Collaboration of the parents, the school, and the child forms the basis of an effective team for designing and implementing an optimal home and school environment for the child. Each member of the team has their own responsibilities and obligations. The home environment fosters the development of social and self-management skills. Parents shape and reinforce the child's self-concept and self-esteem. Without a positive self concept, the child may be resistant to learning and discipline. Consequently, collaboration interventions start at home. The parents are responsible for:

1) Designing an appropriate study area at home.
2) Setting a consistent study time.
3) Providing the school with appropriate documentation, test reports, and information about the child.
4) Providing the school with an appropriate amount of medication.
5) Attending school meetings (parent-teacher conferences, assemblies).
6) Designing a behavioral plan to foster the completion of homework.
7) Praising the child's efforts.
8) Avoiding criticism, sarcasm, and insults when disciplining the child.
9) Allowing the child to experience negative consequences for

19

his\her behavior.

10) Fostering a home environment which is structured and stable.

11) Instructing and reinforcing of appropriate social skills.

Teachers and school personnel are obligated by the law and the profession to provide the "best and most appropriate" education for children. There are laws, such as Section 504 and the Individuals with Disabilities Education Act, which define the role and responsibilities of the school in the education of children with special learning and behavior needs. However, there are some basic principles that "excellent" teachers should apply in the education of children with ADD. The following is a list which describes these general responsibilities of teachers:

l) Designing a classroom environment in which the child can learn.

2) Providing instruction which is interactive and enjoyable.

3) Selecting classroom materials which are of high interest for for all children.

4) Designing and posting classroom expectations, rules, consequences, and rewards.

5) Developing a behavior management system which is accepting and understanding of the child's disability.

6) Testing the child's understanding of the material rather than disability. Timed tests in noisy environments are inappropriate for the child with ADD.

7) Praising the child's efforts. Concentrate on the "goods" rather than criticize the "bads".

8) Centering instruction so it meets all the children's needs rather than the needs of the one.

9) Avoiding statements which bring attention to the child's disability : "Did you take your medication today?"

10) Accepting and understanding the child's disability.

11) Providing appropriate accommodations for the child within the classroom.

The last and most important member of the team is the child. If the child does not desire to change or improve his/her behavior, the "best" interventions and plans which are designed by the parents and teacher are destined to fail. The child should be given opportunities to learn about ADD, its characteristics, causes, treatments, and outcomes. Whether through video, books, or therapists, the information should be presented in forms that the child can understand and retain. The child needs to understand that he\she has responsibilities for their own choices and decisions. Consequently, the child needs to receive consequences for both "good" and "bad" behavioral choices. Without holding the child accountable, he\she may develop inappropriate social skills and habits. These inappropriate skills may lead to more severe emotional and\or behavioral disorders. Therefore, the child has the responsibility of being an active student who provides his\her "best" efforts at home and school. In other words, the child is responsible for:

1) Putting forward his/her "best" effort.
2) Understanding what attention deficit disorder is and is not. It is a real disorder which will effect learning and behavior, however, ADD is not an excuse or reason for failure.
3) Understanding the purpose and importance of his\her medication.
4) Making every effort to remember the medication and accepting help from teacher and parents when he/she forgets it.
5) Accepting of the teacher, content, and skills that are being taught in the class.
6) Accepting and understanding both positive and negative consequences for their behavior.

Individual Learning Plan
An Example of Collaboration

The individual learning plan is a simple, yet structured, tool which fosters the cooperation of the parents, the teacher, and the child in order to improve performance at home and school. The individual learning plan (ILP) is a document which is co-authored by all the members of the team. The ILP is similar to an Individual Education Plan which is mandated under law, The Individuals with Disabilities Education Act, and Section 504. The ILP may provide the foundation for an Individual Education Plan (IEP) or a Section 504 Accommodation Plan. Because it is based on collaboration, the ILP encourages a positive partnership with the schools rather than a "forced" partnership under legal requirements. Unfortunately, there are times at which legal interventions may be appropriate. However, the first steps, which are based upon the ILP, may develop a cooperative rather than adversarial relationships. The document contains several sections, Goal Statement, Individual Strengths, Individual Weaknesses, Parent Responsibilities, Child Responsibilities, School Accommodations, Rewards and Consequences, and signatures. Examples of an outline of an ILP (Appendix C) and completed ILP samples for child (Appendix D) and adolescent (Appendix E) are included in this book.

This document or "contract" encourages the child and parent to cooperate in the setting of goals and rewards\consequences. The child and parent arrange a time to discuss what the child wants to achieve during a specific time period (school year, semester, month, or week). The goals are written in behavioral terms which are measurable. For example, the child will complete 85 of the homework assignments. These goals are designed by the child and agreed upon by the child with assistance of the parents. Then, the parent and child, using test reports and self-reports, write a section on the child's strengths and weaknesses in both learning and behavior. The next section, Parent Responsibilities, is written by the parents to state what they will do to assist their child to achieve the ILP goals at school and home. Then, the child will write (or dictate) what he\she will do to achieve the ILP goals at home and school. The parents and the child co-write the consequences and rewards for completing and achieving their goals. Afterwards, an appointment is arranged with the teacher at the child's school. The child, parents, and teacher discuss the ILP's goals and responsibilities. The teacher is asked to design appropriate accommodations, instruction, and behavior plans which would assist the child in achieving his\her goals for the time period. These accommodations are included in this plan. In addition, individual terms for the revising of the ILP are discussed at the first meeting and generally agreed upon by the members. At the completion of the meeting, the parents, teacher, and child sign and date the document and copies are made for each member of the team. By working together, an environment is created which encourages open communication, clear expectations, and positive interactions between the members.

Treatment Interventions for Children with ADD

The fields of behavioral medicine (psychiatry), psychology, and education offer parents and children with ADD many options for the intervention and treatment. Usually, these options are combined in order to address all the difficulties and issues related to this difference. Interventions are based upon medical management, psychological counseling, and psychoeducational approaches.

Medication Interventions

Children with ADD may benefit from medications which are designed to stabilize the biochemical balance within the brain. Consequently, medications may improve children's abilities to attend, concentrate, focus, and behave. It has been shown through research that approximately 70% of children with ADD show improvement in behavior while on medication. The classes of medications which are usually prescribed to address ADD are psychostimulants and tricyclic antidepressants. When a child is placed on medication, it is critical that the physician who prescribes the medication monitors the child's performance on a regular basis. A Medication Monitoring Checklist (Appendix F) is included in this book. This sheet may be copied and used by the parent to assist in the monitoring of medication.

Psychostimulants

For children with ADD, psychostimulants usually enable the child to better focus, improves visual motor coordination, decreases motor activity, and improves more goal-oriented behavior. Commonly prescribed psychostimulants are Ritalin (methylphenidate), Dexedrine (d-amphetamine), and Cylert (pemoline).

Ritalin is the most commonly prescribed medication for ADD. In general, children who are on Ritalin, show improvement within thirty to ninety minutes after ingestion. The medication usually works for three to five hours, therefore, several doses may be required throughout the day. Sometimes, children who are on Ritalin experience a rebound effect which occurs after the last dose of the day. This effect, which is due to withdrawal from medication, may result in the child temporarily displaying more exaggerated symptoms, such as hyperactivity, sensitivity, and irritability than originally seen in the child. The rebound effect occurs randomly and may be related to external stresses such as school or peer conflicts. Ritalin, which is taken two to four times per day, is usually prescribed in 5, 10, 20 and 20-SR (slow release) doses. The amount of the dosage may be based upon body chemistry, severity of the characteristics, and other medical conditions.

Dexedrine is the second type of psychostimulant which is used to address ADD. Because of the medical procedures which are required to prescribe this medication, it is not used as often. The potential benefits and side effects of Dexedrine and Ritalin are similar.

Cylert, which is sometimes used when Ritalin is not appropriate, has an advantage of a long time of action. Usually, children on Cylert start at 37.5 milligrams once a day. The disadvantage of Cylert is that it usually takes several weeks to take effect.

The common side effects of psychostimulants may include the following: appetite reduction, sleep difficulties, headaches, nausea, irritability, and constipation. Additionally, movement disorders, such as tics, may appear in a small percentage of the children who are on psychostimulants. Given the severity of these side effects, a psychostimulant may be discontinued and other medication may be employed. The current medical research suggests that prolonged use of psychostimulants will not effect a child's growth.

Some physicians believe that ADD is a "school disability," not a life disability. Consequently, these physicians prescribe only medication during school hours. Since the effects of most psychostimulants last from three to four hours, the child taking medication during school hours may be in control for half the day and out of control for the other half of the day. Since the child will not be on medication during family time, the child, parents, and siblings are placed on a medication "yo-yo" which may hinder or impair the child's academic and social development and the family's cohesion. In the author's opinion, if a child benefits from medication during school hours, it is humane to both parents and child to allow the child the medication during non-school hours. This decision may be based upon the severity of ADD and the demands of the child's home environment.

Tricyclic Antidepressants

In some cases where psychostimulants have not been successful or their side effects are too severe, tricyclic antidepressants may be used. The most commonly prescribed antidepressants for children with ADD are Tofranil (Imipramine) and Norpramin (Desipramine).

The advantages of these medications are that they can be taken once a day before bed and can work almost round the clock. They rarely cause appetite suppression or insomnia and can reduce hyperactivity. The disadvantages of these medications are that they will not improve a child's ability to focus or concentrate. They take three to four weeks to have any noticeable effect. Sometimes Ritalin and an antidepressant are used to improve concentration, lessen hyperactivity, and minimize aggression and/or sadness. These two medications may cause significant side effects. The side effects may include the following: constipation, dry mouth, elevated blood pressure, confusion, or manic-like behavior. Consequently, these medications must be monitored carefully.

Psychological Interventions

Children with ADD commonly have associated or secondary emotional or family problems that are the result of the disorder. Because ADD is a biochemical disorder, professionals generally agree that emotional or environmental factors do not cause ADD, but may exaggerate or worsen its symptoms. However, depression or anxiety disorders can "mimic" the symptoms of ADD or secondary ADD. These children with a primary emotional disorder and secondary ADD generally do not have a "true" ADD and may not respond to treatments which are commonly employed for ADD. Consequently, an accurate diagnosis and consistent follow-up may avoid a misdiagnosis and inappropriate treatment. With this in mind, psychological interventions provide a flexible approach to address emotional, social, and family problems regardless of the diagnosis.

The purpose of therapy is not to "cure" the disorder but to provide a setting which will assist the parents and the child in addressing specific family problems and issues, such as discipline and communication. A therapist may provide useful information and insight on parenting skills which may assist the parents in coping with the child's disorder. At times, the child may develop emotional or behavioral difficulties that are not directly related to ADD. For example, whether ADD or not, a child may develop significant emotional and/or behavioral problems due to a parents' divorce, a death in the family, or physical or sexual abuse. Consequently, the purpose of therapy would be to provide a safe setting for the child to share their emotions or issues and to discover effective ways to express these feelings. A therapist should have an understanding of ADD and how this disorder will affect the child's behavior and emotions; however, the focus of therapy is not on ADD, but on the child's current behavioral and/or emotional problems. The effectiveness of therapy is usually based upon the willingness and cooperation of the parents and the child. Like the old saying, "you get out of it what you put into it," therapy "works" only when the individuals work together to solve their problems.

Psychological interventions are commonly employed using the following three approaches: individual, group, and family. These interventions are usually performed by a "licensed" professional; psychologist, psychiatrist or social worker. Individual therapy is generally more intense and directed toward the child's emotional and behavioral difficulties. The sessions may focus on the expression of the child's emotional issues. Once confronted with these issues, the therapist and the child work together in finding an appropriate method to understand and possibly eliminate those issues. Using a wide range of therapeutic approaches, the therapist provides the child a safe environment to explore their frustration, anger, sadness, or confusion because of the disorder.

Group therapy is designed to foster group problem solving and self exploration with four to twelve children or adolescents. Allowing the children to work together under a structure, rules, and expectations, the therapist (and co-therapist) encourages the group to discuss specific topics, to provide feedback to group members, and to support group members through crises. Unlike individual sessions, group therapy may pose some unique challenges to children with ADD. Because they are not the focus of the therapist's complete attention, the child with ADD may compete with other children for more time to talk or may "drift off" or daydream when other group members are talking. A group therapy session may create an environment which may encourage some of the same behavioral problems that children with ADD face in school settings.

Finally, family therapy, which is commonly conducted by social workers, may address the dynamics and issues of the "whole" family. A family therapist may require the child with ADD, the parents or guardians, siblings and possibly relatives, to participate in the sessions. A therapist may foster appropriate communication skills between parents and children, in order to establish structure and enhance self-esteem. Rules, expectations, and discipline are major topics for parents with children who are diagnosed with ADD. The therapist may provide feedback and guidance to the family in the resolution of specific issues which are confronting the family.

The option of counseling is somewhat questionable because these children may have difficulties with talking about their issues and understanding conversations. Children with ADD usually are poor historians, that is, they have difficulty in remembering, understanding and explaining their past. Furthermore, they tend to misinterpret other's statements and questions and mis-state their ideas and feelings, and interrupt the flow of the session with unrelated thoughts and questionable feedback.

Psychoeducational Interventions

A psychoeducation approach utilizes psychological principles of dealing with feelings and emotions and employs educational techniques to instruct children on how to improve their social and educational skills. This approach stresses the building of proper adult-child relationships that can promote emotional development in the context of social and academic skill improvement. In other words, the instructor teaches children "how to go to school" and "how to live in a family." Within this context, the instructor may provide enhancement and remediation of educational and language difficulties which may have hindered development of oral language (listening and speaking) and written language (reading and writing) skills. Generally, these programs, which may be taught by a special education teacher, social worker, psychologist, or a mental health professional, are based upon a class outline or syllabus. In each session a different topic may be introduced that would enhance the development or the reinforcement of appropriate social or educational skills. The following is an example of a psychoeducation class schedule:

Week 1: Introductions, magic words and class rules.
Week 2: Consequences and Responsibilities.
Week 3: Conversation and Friendship skills.
Week 4: Handling anger and frustration.
Week 5: Sportsmanship and sharing skills.
Week 6: Personal hygiene and table manners.
Week 7: School skills-asking questions, asking for help.
Week 8: School skills-Homework and test taking.

While the children are learning these skills, the parents may be enrolled in classes on ADD, parenting, and school relations. The parents learn how to better manage their child with as little stress as possible. In addition, parents are exposed to school law and the rights and responsibilities of the school and the parents in the educating of their children. Furthermore, the parents may learn about ADD, its traits, causes, diagnosis, and treatments. Special sessions are arranged with nurses and/or physicians to discuss medication usage and monitoring.

One advantage to this approach is that it provides direct instruction and remediation of social and language skills through role modeling and real life experiences. By developing these skills, children with ADD may be able to effectively and appropriately interact with peers and adults. Another advantage of the psychoeducation approach is that it provides an interactive and "entertaining" environment where they can learn skills that are generally assumed to be learned. Because social and behavioral skills are rarely directly taught in school settings, children with ADD, due to their behavioral traits, may have a significant difficulty in learning and applying these skills at home and school. Their teachers and parents "assume" that these children will understand, apply, and generalize social and behavioral skills. The psychoeducation approach does not make this assumption, therefore, all sessions are taught very overtly. By directly teaching these children how to "appropriately" interact with parents, teachers, and peers, their self-esteem may be enhanced and their behavior may be improved.

Psychiatric Interventions

In cases of severe emotional or behavioral disorders, psychiatric care may be appropriate. The hospitalization of children is usually a traumatic event; thus, this option should be used only after other interventions have failed. Under the care of child and adolescent psychiatrists, social workers, nurses, psychologists, activity therapists, and teachers, children in this setting receive intense individual, group, and family therapy. Using medication and therapeutic interventions, the psychiatric setting may assist the family through the crisis providing guidance and support through various treatment options.

Conclusion

In the beginning of this book, readers were introduced to Jimmy, a child with ADD. Every day, Jimmy's self-esteem is hurt and diminished. Without appropriate interventions, educationally and psychologically, Jimmy may be at risk for developing further, deeper emotional disorders. All Jimmy may need is one caring adult to show him how to succeed at school and behave at home. Just one adult to take the time and effort to teach Jimmy how to rise from the educational and emotional ashes of ADD and achieve his dreams. As an adult with both ADD and dyslexia, I was fortunate to have professionals assist me to discover my talents and abilities. My deepest wish for the children with ADD is that they have the same "real chance" to find their own special and unique gifts.

With loving parents, supportive teachers, and understanding friends, children with ADD may flourish with success and happiness. Individuals with ADD may be one of the greatest untapped and misunderstood treasures in our schools, work places and homes.

Appendix A - F

Appendix A

Parent's Guide to Intelligence and Educational Tests

Intelligence

Wechsler Intelligence Scales for Children - III
*This test measures the child's verbal and performance (nonverbal) intelligence. (Wechsler, D. 1991, The Psychological Corporation)

Detroit Tests of Learning Aptitude - 3
*This test measures the child's intelligence and cognition. (Hammill, D. 1991, American Guidance Services)

Woodcock Johnson - Revised Tests of Cognitive Abilities
*This test measures the child's cognitive abilities; oral language, processing speed, reasoning, perceptual-motor skills, and learning abilities. (Woodcock, J. and Johnson, M. 1988, DLM Teaching Resources)

Kaufman Brief Intelligence Test
*This test provides a quick estimate or measure of intelligence and cognition. (Kaufman, A. and Kaufman, N. 1990, American Guidance Services.)

Educational and Language

Woodcock Johnson - Revised Tests of Achievement
*This test measures reading, mathematics, written language, and knowledge. (Woodcock, R. and Johnson, M. 1989 DLM Teaching Resources)

Test of Written Language - 2
*This test measures written language; paragraph writing, sentence writing, spelling, and grammar. (Hammill, D. and Larsen, S. 1988, Pro - Ed)

Test of Language Competence - Expanded Edition
*This test measures oral language, both receptive and expressive language skills. It also assesses the child is social comprehension and skills. (Wiig, E. and Secord, W. 1988, The Psychological Corporation)

Test of Written Spelling - 2
   *This test assesses the child's spelling skills for regular (phonetic) and irregular words. (Larsen, S. and Hammill, D. 1986 Pro - Ed)

Lindamood Test of Auditory Conceptualization
   *This test measures the child's ability to understand sound-letter relationships. (Lindamood, C. and Lindamood, P. 1979 DLM Teaching Resources)

Goldman-Fristoe-Woodcock Selective Auditory Attention Test
   *This test measures the child's ability to attend, focus, and discriminate directions in noisy (distracting) environments. (Goldman, R., Fristoe, M., and Woodcock, R. 1974, American Guidance Services)

Peabody Picture Vocabulary Test - Revised
   *This test measures oral vocabulary skills. (Dunn, L., and Dunn, O. 1981, American Guidance Service)

Test of Adolescent Language - 2
   *This test measures an adolescent's abilities using grammar and vocabulary in written and spoken language. (Hammill, D., Brown, V., Larsen, S. and Wiederholt, J. 1987, The Psychological Corporation)

Clinical Evaluation of Language Fundamentals - Revised
   *This test measures the child's oral language abilities. (Semel, E., Wiig, E., and Secord, W. 1987, The Psychological Corporation)

Appendix B

A Parent's Guide to Test Results

Test results are usually presented in three ways; percentile rank, standard score, and age/grade equivalent. A percentile rank and a standard score provide an accurate and appropriate measure of a child's test performance.

Grade/age Equivalents

According to the American Psychological Association and the International Reading Association, these are inappropriate for test usage and interpretations. Unfortunately, grade/age equivalents are used by professionals and parents to "determine" the child's function level. A grade/age equivalent does not indicate at which grade the child is performing. This score only indicates at which grade the child's score is at the 50th percentile rank.

Percentile Rank

A Percentile Rank score describes a child's performance on a scale from 1 to 99 in comparison with the performance of others his/her age. The average percentile rank is 50. If, for example, a child scored at the 65th percentile, it means that 65% of the children of his/her chronological age scored lower and 35% scored higher than the child.

Standard Score

A standard score is a "statistically" based score which provides a comparison of the child's performance to other children his/her age. This score is based on a mean of 100 with a standard deviation of 125. Thus, if your child obtained a standard score of 120, he/she scored in the above average range for his/her age group. If the standard score was 90, he/she performed at the lower end of the average range for his/her age group. If your child obtained a standard score of 120, he/she scored in the above average range for his/her age group.

In the author's opinion, it is "best" to understand the child's test results using percentile ranks. Percentile ranks provide the reader with an appropriate comparison of the child's results in comparison to his/her peer group. It is recommended that parents receive a copy of the test report and have the opportunity to discuss it with a professional.

Appendix C

INDIVIDUAL LEARNING PLAN
Outline

I. Goals for School and Home
  1. Academic Performance
  2. Behavior

II. Individual Strengths
  1. Defined by Child
  2. Defined by Parents

III. Individual Weaknesses
  1. Defined by Child
  2. Defined by Parent

IV. Student Responsibilities

V. Parent Responsibilities

VI. School Assistance and Accommodations

VII. Rewards and Consequences
  1. Positive
  2. Negative

VIII. Signatures
  1. Parents
  2. Child
  3. Teacher

Appendix D

INDIVIDUAL LEARNING PLAN
Elementary Version

Name:	Brian Jones	Grade:	Fourth	Age:	Nine

I. Goals for School (Behavior and Achievement)
- A. Behavior:
  1. As described by teachers:
     - a. Will raise hand before speaking.
     - b. Will keep hands and feet to himself.
     - c. Will work on assignments in class and not disturb others.
     - d. Will stay in his seat when his teacher is teaching.
     - e. Will do his share in groups.
  2. As described by Brian.
     - a. I will finish my work in my classroom, and if I don't, I will take it home to finish. I need help to remember to take it home.
     - b. I will work harder on multiplication
     - c. I will try to be a better listener so that I can remember directions given by the teacher.
     - d. I will ask for directions if I don't understand what I am to do.
     - e. I will try not to talk to the other kids when they are working.
     - f. I will carry a separate notebook to draw in. I must have time to draw. It helps me relax. I will try not to draw on my assignment papers.
     - g: I will return books to school on a timely basis.
- B. Achievement:
  1. Brian will receive the same assignment as his peers and will be expected to work, without playing, for the allotted work time. His teacher will determine additional time needed on the assignment and will note it in the assignment book.
  2. Spelling, math, and reading assignments will not be modified.

3. Computer: Appropriate usage by Brian
4. Science and Social Studies: expected to participate with his fourth grade peers.
5. All assignments in his assignment book are due the following day unless otherwise noted.

II. Individual Strengths
   A. I am a good artist with my own style.
   B. I am a good friend.
   C. I have a good sense of humor.
   D. I like my new teacher.

III. Individual Weaknesses
   A. I am not good at getting along with most of my teachers.
   B. I have a hard time finishing my work because they give me too much to do and I don't have time to finish it all.

IV. Student Responsibilities
   A. I will clean my desk once a week, on Friday.
   B. I will try as hard as I can to learn and behave properly.
   C. I will work one hour every day, except Thursday, at home. One half hour on reading and the other finishing school assignments or working on multiplication.
   D. I will follow classroom rules.

V. Parent Responsibilities
   A. I will structure school preparations at home so Brian can arrive in the classroom as calm as possible.
   B. I will praise good choices and small accomplishments.
   C. I will provide a quiet place for Brian to do his homework.
   D. I will try to remain cheerful in the face of setbacks and Brian's negative attitudes.
   E. I will try to find a structured, out-of-school activity, that Brian can participate in.

VI. School Accommodations
   A. Classroom Accommodations.
      1. Minimize classroom distraction from classmates.
      2. Locate seat near the teacher's desk.
      3. Locate seat away from hallway and windows.
      4. Post schedule and routine daily.
   B. Instructional Accommodations
      1. Vary the speed of the lessons.

2. Design brief lessons.
3. Employ multisensory instructional methods.
   a. Instruct the child to develop mental images.
   b. Use role playing activities to act out key concepts.
   c. Use cooperative learning activities with preassigned roles and responsibilities.
   d. Maintain frequent eye contact with the child during verbal instructions.
   e. Make directions clear and concise. Be consistent with directions.
   f. Simplify complex directions. Avoid directions with several steps.
   g. Assess the child's comprehension of directions before beginning the task.
   h. Repeat directions in a calm, positive manner when necessary.
C. Testing and Home/School Work Accommodations
   1. Shorten assignments.
   2. Provide an environment which is distraction free when the child is completing a test.
   3. Provide extended time for the child to complete the test.
   4. Allow the child the opportunity, when necessary, to take tests orally or in an alternative method papers and projects.
D. Organizational Accommodations
   1. Use individual assignment charts or homework sheets which are sent home to the parent.
   2. Develop a clear system for tracking homework, completed, incomplete, and missing assignments. These sheets may be sent home to parent.
   3. Develop a reward system for in-school work and homework completion.
   4. Write schedule and time lines for assignments and projects on board.
   5. Prepare the child for changes in activities by announcing to the class when current activity is ending.
E. Behavioral Accommodations

1. Class rules ought to be clear and simple.
2. Have the class agree on what the rules should be.
3. Define and review classroom rules each day at the start of the school year.

VII. Rewards and Consequences (If appropriate)
   A. At school
      1. Rewards
         a. School
            l) Computer during band and strings time.
            2) Praise for completed assignments.
         b. Home
            l) If Brian completes his assignments for the week (reduced work load) and shows real effort, he can have a friend over or another arrangement to be decided at the time.
            2) If Brian works well at home with no complaining, he can have the rest of the evening free.
      2. Consequences
         a. School
            l) Finish incomplete assignments during band and strings time.
            2) 1,2,3 behavior management system
         b. Home
            l) If he doesn't work well, there are always chores to do around the house and no television viewing.

VIII. Signatures
I have read the plan and agree with its implementation.

NAME   **TITLE**

_____

_____

_____

_____

_____

Appendix E

Individual Learning Plan

1. Goals for School (behavior and achievement)

The grades I received last Year: The grades I want to achieve this year:
(That are acceptable)

The grades I received last Year:		The grades I want to achieve this year: (That are acceptable)	
English	D	English	C
Math	C	Math	C or better
Social Studies	C	Social Studies	C or better
Science	B	Science	B or better
Spanish	D	Spanish	C or better
Suspensions	5	Suspensions	2 or less
Detentions	10	Detentions	5 or less

- It is reasonable to expect that I may improve in some subjects while not in others. As long as I am trying my hardest and my grades do not slip below a D in any subject, it is acceptable.

- Last year I was suspended from school five times. This year I will not exceed two suspensions, if any. As long as what I got in trouble for was not serious enough to warrant being expelled, my parents will consider this an improvement.

- Last year I was given detention ten times for being tardy to class. This year I will only receive a maximum of five detentions.

- I will miss no more than one homework assignment per week.

- I will try not to talk as much during class, and obey each teacher's rules.

2. Individual Strengths

- I am good at science.

- I am good at writing

3. Individual Weaknesses

- I have a hard time keeping track of my assignments.

- I am not as good at spelling.

4. Student Responsibilities

- I am committed to put forth my best effort towards school work and the proper school behavior.

- I will find a quiet place with few distractions for studying.

- I will set a block of time each day to study, and sit in this place for at least one hour and read if I have no work to finish for that day. I understand this is to help me become used to having a study place, and I will not complain when I have no homework to accomplish.

- I will try to keep my desk neater than last year, so the teacher does not "dump my desk".

- I will follow the rules of each teacher to the best of my ability.

- I will bring home books, homework, and folders relevant to my school assignments each day.

- I will keep a calendar of assignments in plain view in the home.

- I will not become angry when my parents ask to see my homework, because I know that they are trying to help me be a better student, and they care about me.

5. Parent Responsibilities

- I will provide a distraction-free place for my child to study (where possible) and set times for his/her completion of work.

- I will try, to the best of my ability, to review my child's completed homework.

- I will provide a calendar and instruct my child in its use to organize assignments and tests, as well as social and extracurricular activities.

- I will try, to the best of my ability, to be encouraging where possible, and will not become angry when my child has negative progress or falls short of meeting his/her goals.

- I agree that my temporary setbacks regarding my responsibilities are allowed because of unforeseen situation, but that continued nonsupport will be a violation of this agreement.

6. **School Accommodations (refer to book section, School Accommodations)**

7. **Rewards and Consequences (if appropriate)**

   - If I spend my block of time studying and my work on my assignments and projects are complete, I can go about my business for the rest of the day.

   - If I have not completed my assignments and projects, I will not be allowed to watch T.V. that night, nor will I be allowed to play with my friends that day. Extracurricular activities?

   - If I bring home my homework each day for the week of   , I will receive an extra half hour to stay up past my bed time to watch T.V. a certain night.

8. **Signatures**

   We all agree that this contract and its rules will be followed for the current year.

_____   _____
Parent   **Date**   **Parent**   **Date**

              _____
              Child or Adolescent   **Date**

Appendix F

Medication Monitoring Checklist

Child's Name _____ Physician _____

Birthdate _____ Age_____ Sex: M_____ F_____

Parents _____ Date _____

Instructions: This checklist should be completed by parents of children taking psychostimulant medication.

1. Medication: _____Dose: _____
   Frequency:_____

   Medication:_____ Dose: _____
   Frequency: _____

2. Have you noticed any of the following side effects this week: (Circle "X" when the side effect was present).

	SU	MO	TU	WE	TH	FR	SA
• loss of appetite/weight	X	X	X	X	X	X	X
• insomnia	X	X	X	X	X	X	X
• irritability in late morning or late afternoon	X	X	X	X	X	X	X
• unusual crying	X	X	X	X	X	X	X
• tics or nervous habits	X	X	X	X	X	X	X
• headache/stomachache	X	X	X	X	X	X	X
• sadness	X	X	X	X	X	X	X
• rashes	X	X	X	X	X	X	X
• dizziness	X	X	X	X	X	X	X
• fearfulness	X	X	X	X	X	X	X
• social withdrawal	X	X	X	X	X	X	X
• drowsiness	X	X	X	X	X	X	X
• anxiety	X	X	X	X	X	X	X

3. Describe how often and when the side effects occurred:

_____

4. How is the child performing in school?

_____

5. Has your child refused or complained about taking the medication?

_____

6. Have there been any problems with giving the medication at school?

_____

SELECTED REFERENCES ON ATTENTION DEFICIT DISORDER

Classroom and Curriculum Modifications

Chalmers, L. (1992). *Modifying Curriculum for the Special Needs Student in the Regular Classroom.* Practical Press, P.O. Box 455, Moorhead, MN, 56561-0455, (218) 236-5244.

Copeland, E.D. and Love, V.L. (1990). *Attention without Tension: A Teacher's Handbook.* A.D.D. Warehouse, 300 Northwest 70th Avenue, Suite 102, Plantation, FL, 33317, (305) 792-8944.

Harwell, J.M. (1989). *Complete Learning Disabilities Handbook: Ready-to-use Techniques for Teaching Learning Handicapped Students.* The Center for Applied Research in Education, New York: Simon and Schuster.

McCarney, S.B. (1989). *The Attention Deficit Disorders Intervention Manual.* Hawthorne Educational Services, Inc., 800 Gray Oak Drive, Columbia, MO, 65201, (314) 874-1710.

Meltzer, L. and Solomon, B. (1988). *Educational Prescriptions for the Classroom for Students with Learning Problems.* Educators Publishing Service, Inc., 75 Moulton Street, Cambridge, MA, 0213801104.

Paine, S.C. et al. (1992). *Structuring your Classroom for Academic Success: Managing an Elementary Classroom on a Day-to-Day Basis.*

Parker, H. (1992). *The ADD Hyperactivity Handbook for Schools.* Plantation, FL. Impact Publications, Inc.

Wunderlich, K.C. (1988). *The Teacher's Guide to Behavioral Interventions: Intervention Strategies for Behavior Problems in the Educational Environment.* Hawthorne Educational Services, In., 800 Gray Oak Drive, Columbia, MO, 65201, (314) 874-1710.

Study Skills

Dooley, Beverly and Redington, Nancy (1990). *Study Skills Curriculum: Multisensory Study Skills.* EPS, 1129 Garden Gate Circle, Garland, TX, 75043, (214) 272-4862. (Has mapping and time organization sheets.)

Mangrum, Charles T. II, Ed.D. (1983). *Learning to Study: Study Skills/Study Strategies,* (Series A=H). Jamestown Publishers, P.O. Box 6743, Providence, RI. 02940.

Weiss, Martin. (1979). *The Basic Language Kit.* Treehouse Associates, Great Barrington, MA.

Laws

Anderson, W., Chitwood, S., and Hayden, D. (1990). *Negotiating the special education maze.* Rockville, M.D., Woodbine House.

General References

Goldstein, S. & Goldstein, M. (1990). *Managing Attention Disorders in Children: A Guide for Practitioners.* New York, N.Y. Wiley Interscience.

Braswell, L. & Bloomquist, M. (1991). *Cognitive - Behavioral Therapy with ADHD Children: Child, Family, and School Interventions.* New York, N.Y. The Guildford Press.

Moss, R. (1990). *Why Johnny Can't Concentrate.* New York, N.Y. Bantam Books.

Wender, P. (1987). *The Hyperactive Child, Adolescent, and Adult: Attention Deficit Disorder through the Lifespan.* New York, N.Y. Oxford University Press.

Barkley, R. (1990). *Attention Deficit Disorder: A Handbook for Diagnosis and Treatment.* New York, N.Y., Guilford Press.

Freidman, R. & Doyal, G. (1992). *Management of Children and Adolescents with Attention Deficit Hyperactivity Disorder.* Austin, TX. Pro-Ed, Inc.

Silver, L. (1992). *Attention Deficit Hyperactivity Disorder: A Clinical Guide to Diagnosis and Treatment.* Washington, D.C. The American Psychiatric Press.

Silver, L. (1992). *Dr. Larry Silver's Advice to Parents on Attention Deficit Hyperactivity Disorder.* Washington, D.C. The American Psychiatric Press.

Ingersoll, B. (1988). *Your Hyperactive Child: A Parent's Guide to Coping with Attention Deficit Disorder.* New York, N.Y. Doubleday, Inc.

Attention Deficit Disorder Video

Phelan, T. (1990). *1-2-3 Magic: Training Preschooler and Preteen to do What You Want Them to do.* Carol Stream, IL, Child Management.

Phelan, T. (1990). *All About Attention Deficit Disorder.* Carol Stream, IL. Child Management.

Goldstein, S. (1991). *It's Just Attention Disorder,* Salt Lake City, UT. Neurology, Learning, and Behavior Center.

The majority of these books and materials are available through the Add Warehouse, 300 Northwest 70th Avenue, Suite 102, Plantation, FL   33317 - Phone (305) 792-8944.